there's nothing better than
the company of night —
it's when our most
intense thoughts come out to play

— the night owl

S.P. BURRELL & DAVIA CHIN

Up All Night

A POETIC COLLECTION OF
LATE NIGHT THOUGHTS.

Up All Night
A Poetic Collection of Late Night Thoughts
Copyright © 2021 S.P. Burrell and Davia Chin

Illustrations by Davia Chin

ISBN: 9798456284273
ISBN: 978-1-7375096-3-9

10 9 8 7 6 5 4 3 2
Printed in the United States

Priceless Publishing®
Coral Springs, Fl
www.pricelesspublishing.co

dedication

We would like to dedicate this book to our moms, Dwinette Davis and Carlene Burrell. Thank you for bringing us into this world, being the center of our lives, and our greatest source of inspiration.

contents

acknowledgment

I would like to thank Essence, who has not only been an amazing coworker but a great friend. You've been the one who has listened to me consistently, and without judgement. Regardless of how crazy I felt, I could always count on you for encouragement. You're always the first person to read my books, listen to my songs, and support me. It's hard to find people like you in the world! Thank you for being an inspiration and such a true friend.

— S.P. Burrell

I want to thank the incredible people in my life: To my spouse, thank you for your incredible patience and unwavering support — our love is the light that brightens my life. To my mother, who is my greatest inspiration and reason for being — thank you for always believing in me. To my son and brother, my uncle and grandmother, sisters Q and S.P — thank you for transforming a dull year of quarantine and making it beautiful. To all my family, well-wishers, publishing team, and readers — thank you for your support.

— Davia Chin

PART I

4am thoughts

—

we spend
days and nights
thinking about
what we want,
but do we know
that if we just
listened to that voice
in the back
of our minds
it would guide us
exactly where we
needed to go?

—the subconscious

wandering souls
have no home,
no place to go,
they leave a piece
of themselves
everywhere they go
passing through just
as fast as they came
they continually seek
for what is missing
inside of themselves -
trying to fill the void
only makes it grow,
so the wanderers
are left to
keep searching
even when
there's nothing there

—finding a purpose

sometimes,

it's tiring
when you must
watch the people
in your life
come and go

sometimes,

you wonder
if they can stay

a little while longer,

to make your life
just a little bit brighter

but then you realize,

that you need to
let them go
they've served

their purpose,

helped you learn
your lesson
there's no reason
to keep them

in your life,

and no matter
how hard you try
the universe
just won't let you

— struggling to let go

how far
are you
willing to go
to find your dream,
to save yourself
from becoming
something unknown?

— taking a leap of faith

i close my eyes,
imagining a glowing window
in front of me —
a portal that would take
me anywhere
i want to go

the first and only
place i wish to go
is where i'm shrouded
in peace and happiness,
staring into the face
of the reality
i dream of everyday,

the paradise that slowly
created itself
inside my mind
i hold the hand
of the human
who loves me the most,

i breathe the air,
feel the sunshine,
the wind on my skin
melting into the feeling
of pure bliss,
i drift into a deep sleep
knowing that paradise

will come to me soon

— finding my paradise

sometimes,
we feel
that we belong
to no one

our hearts
are empty,
drained from
the ones who claim
to love us

when should
we feel
like we belong
to ourselves

every night
i dream,
so real and vivid

they take me
away from reality
it's so real,
i still feel
the emotions
swirling inside me
when i wake
i want to stay —
i need to stay
inside the world
that i have created

i need to breathe
the air
in a place
where i'm safe
and free
from the life
that consumes me
when i'm awake

— lucid dreaming

imagine
all that we
could accomplish
if we just told ourselves
that we can do anything

when my thoughts
wander inside
my mind,
each one stops
just for a moment

as i focus,
it floats away
until another
takes its place

— sitting alone in
the dark

we are lost —
all of us,
are lost

some of us
know what we're
searching for,
but don't know
how to get there

some of us
don't know
where to start,
as the journey
is too daunting,
too risky,
to bring anything
we want
into fruition

a girl
trapped inside
her own mind
is dangerous —
she fears nothing
except

her own thoughts,
which plague her
to the point
of self-destruction

her will
is so powerful
she could destroy
anyone,
but instead,
she chooses
to destroy herself

— she needs no one

the biggest question
that i ask myself every day is —
why?
why do i end up
giving people
more than they give me?

why?
why has the world
made human beings
so cruel,
that the only thing
that they know

is how to take from others?

it's so hard
to find
the humans
that are good
when the bad ones
are everywhere…

—fighting my
codependence

my mind is my kingdom
my heart — the ruler
my soul — the glue
that holds it together

when i fall apart
i feel as if
a war is coming,
and if i don't fight
the kingdom
that i've built
will be destroyed

the thoughts that run
through my mind,
i wish i could capture,
write all of them down

so impossible —
they float continuously
through the endless sea,
only to return
when i am most pensive

— drowning in my
thoughts

how do you erase
the painful memories,
the guilt
of bad decisions,
the mistakes,
that keep you
awake at night?

,

i wonder
what it's like
to explore
the vast emptiness
of another planet

just to imagine
the way it feels
to have that emptiness
inside of yourself

— life on mars

walking through the forest
of your broken dreams
you find that
your emotions

get the best of you

you wonder
what could have been
if only these dreams
could have been real,
how different
your life could be,
maybe you could change
as a person

but how
would you ever know,
until you fix them
one by one?

my heart
is always happy
when someone is grateful
because of
something i said
or something i did
for them
there's something about
giving joy to others
that makes life worthwhile

her intense warmth and charm
devours everything in her wake
she is a mystery —

powerful and destructive
she rises with grace
after every conquest,
she overcomes every doubter
they examine her
with keen interest
from a distance
because she is fire
and they will get burned

— empowered woman

must i be a savage
to survive the 21st century?

fraudulently
getting by on your
instagram timeline

why can't i just be me?
a sensitive
imperfect
work in progress?

AM_A_SAVAGE

3,220 likes

sometimes i wonder
if my life were really my own,
with no one to answer to
and no one else's expectation
to live up to but my own
callow judgment —
who would i become?

what do i do now?
where do i go from here?

questions
that perplex my mind
as i come to the realization

that i don't have
all the answers
to the unending mysteries
of my life
i've betrayed my hopes and dreams
my reality is unfamiliar
now buried in a sea of disappointment
because i,
once the most likely to succeed
have failed

but perhaps the goal isn't
perfection,
but progress

i fear the criticism from failure
more than i do failure itself
it is the thought
of others watching me
as i stumble and fall face down
that i find most unbearable

they will recognize my failure,
but will they see
beyond my fall?
will i ever redeem myself
in their eyes?

will they acknowledge
my resilience?

failure does not have to be final
it is within us to learn,
grow,

and evolve

we all say we want
to love and be loved —
we want a love
that could last forever,
one that will stand
the test of time,
a love that
lights our darkness

we yearn for an honest love
with a one
we'll never know entirely
because it's easy to love
the ones we don't know

the hard part is loving ourselves
with whom there are no secrets

i have found no better way
to put my misery to an end
than immortalizing you
with my paper and pen

— the healing power of art

how do i break free from the prison
that is my mind?

commandeering my every thought
in an endless cycle of rumination,
bombarding me with questions
of what if's,

criticizing my actions
with unsolicited advice
and should haves

— overthinking

i am every woman
past, present and future
linked by our femininity

i feel her pain,
i know her fears
her struggles are my own,
so i take pride in her successes
and celebrate her victories

because she is my redeemer —
her feet carry me forward
her strides empower me
and because of her
i know i am capable

i can succeed

— women

boundaries are not:
the rejection of others

boundaries are:
knowing who you are and
staying true to your values

boundaries are:
choosing your happiness and
making yourself the priority

boundaries are:
creating space for your peace
and knowing when to let go

boundaries are:
saying no to the things that do not serve you
while loving from a distance

do opinions matter?

society tells us
that we are all-knowing
so there's no reason to listen
to the opinions of others

but there can be a fine line between
ignorance and knowledge

we are the expert on who we are
and our purpose in the world
self-definition is a personal job

but in matters of life
the wise seek counsel

we live our lives in a rush
attempting to maintain a pace
that is unsustainable
never taking time to slow down
and live in the moment
because we're too afraid

we're afraid that the free time
will make us think,
feel and self-assess

we prefer self-destruction
because slowing down carries
the risk of feeling uncomfortable,
and admitting the truth to ourselves
that we are not where we want to be

— slow down

we take a stroll
on the perfect summer day —

when the sun sits high,
and the wind kisses us gently as it drifts by
when the air is seasoned,
with happiness and laughter
as conversations dance on our lips,
in tune with the rhythm
of our moving hips

we enjoy the sweetness
of an ice cream cone
as it cools us down
from the summer heat
bouncing on our skin...
we capture with our eyes
the beauty of the landscape —

the lush green grass,
the sunflowers waving hello,
the birds playing hide and seek
in the majestic trees

you and i are present
in the moment of bliss
and all is well with the world

in the blink of an eye
clouds choke the sun,
darkening the land
rain showers down,

leaving us wet and exposed,
cold and confused

that is what my anxiety feels like

— anxiety

i thought forgiveness
would be too easy a price
for the undeserving,
so i fought them
fire with fire
until all that was left
of our worlds were ash

i became the monster that i loathe
and hated me for it

love, compassion, and forgiveness
are the acts reserved for
those of us who are brave

— absolution

they say love conquers all
but that must have been
before she encountered ego
and he left her for dead

the most humbling experience in life
is the crushing devastation of death
the loss, hurt and grief
act as crude reminders
that we're not invincible —
time is not ours
we should treasure life
because living is a privilege

i can have all that i desire
i am smart, capable and resourceful
i have the willpower to accomplish
all that I wish

i am committed to self-improvement
every day is a new opportunity for me
to show up as my best self
i am destined to make a difference

— note to self

some days i wake
and find myself stuck
between confident and needing approval

building up and breaking down,
motivated and ready to give up

on those days
i rest, not quit

i love when it rains
the sound of pitter-patter on the roof,
synchronizing to the beat of my heart
whispering words of wisdom
reminding me that there are better days to come,
there is beauty after the storm

— rain and rainbows

why do we shy away
from the things that would most fulfill us
because no one understands our lives vision
or support our dream?

why do we suffocate
our potential—
fitting in places
that we've outgrown?

when will we live our lives
on our terms—
play the game to win

dominate the tracks
in the life's arena
regardless of who
shows up and applauds

— applause

i thought my mind to be
a cruel kingdom
where invasive thoughts reigned
and i was held, hostage
unable to roam free
without the confinement of doubt

until i understood its prowess
harnessed its powers—
imprisoned my doubts and fears,
created worlds of abundance
and infinite possibilities

— point of view

i was buried so deep
i tasted dirt with every breath
it broke me and tore me apart
so wide i could never be whole again

determined to survive
i gripped the earth
with every ounce of my being
and clawed my way through the soil

the brokenness i left behind
has become the roots i now stand on

— flower

my heart's truest display
of resistance
is my stubborn will
to defy vulnerability

if i never open-up
the secret of my soul
can never be revealed

— defiance

PART II

lovelorn

—

broken hearts,
wandering love
hide me from

the truth —

i just can't take
the pain
and dejection
that comes
with love,
nowhere to go
except here,
in my thoughts
please,
let me go

— breaking up with him
again

every human
wants to find love,
wants to be in love,
but they are
so scared
to find it
and scared
to face
what comes with it

i looked into the eyes
of the person i loved
my profound sadness
brought me to tears
as i watched them walk away
never to come back again

i thought of all the ways
i could make them come back
if i changed,
if i were better
maybe they wouldn't
have left me

— there's always someone
who'll never leave

it's so hard
to trust someone
with your heart

you make
yourself vulnerable
hoping that
they'll take
this part

of you
and care for it,
instead of
breaking it

into the pieces
that you'll slowly
have to pick up

because of him
i hate purple

it was the color
of the heart
next to his name
in my phone

heartbreak ensued
i deleted everything,
erased all our memories
now purple only
reminds me of
being broken

— the man who loved me
wrong

i loved them
for who they were
i gave my all
so that our relationship
was easy,
so close to being perfect

i worked so hard,
that i struggled
to be happy
knowing that they
had me
waiting in vain
for what i truly desired

for my own sake,
i let go
and was flooded
with relief
remembering,
that there is always someone else
who would never
make me wait
in order to be happy

— i always knew i deserved
better

love is so difficult
to understand

one day
you find yourself
in a relationship
and you feel as if

you finally understand

what it feels like
then,

things end —
you move on
without them,
and love starts to become
a mind-bending mystery
once again

being left behind hurts,
being betrayed
hurts even more,
knowing that
they didn't care
enough about you
to even try

meet me at
the end of the world
and we can start over together

— genesis

i've wasted so much
of my time
believing in
the false promises
of those who claimed
that they loved and cared for me

— deleting phone numbers

in the late of night
a doubt forms in my mind
making my restless

i feel like i won't find
the one who loves me the most,
the one who'll give me better,
the human whose love
will overpower
everything that i had
previously believed

i feel as if they are
just a wandering thought,
a visualization
that will never come into
existence

— where is the one?

my first love
was a man
in his 30's
he charmed me,
loved me,

told me how much
he wanted to get married,
to build a family with me

he raved about how
i was so different
from the other women
he'd dated
how i was the first one
to stay with him
as he went
through difficult times,
how i was the woman
who loved him unconditionally,
and made life easier for him,
with no baggage or constant drama

how unfair,
that the man i loved so much
would be so grateful
for the gift of
an easy and effortless
relationship with me,
when he failed miserably
to provide
the same for me,
doing the complete opposite
of what i constantly did for him

i spent nights crying over
how he emotionally drained me,
how he came into my life
and made it so difficult,
that i constantly
thought of leaving him,
just to free myself from
the drama he dragged me into,
the baggage that he constantly
brought into our relationship
until it was ruined —
until i was so unhappy,
that nothing he could do
would stop me from leaving

i would look in the mirror,
ashamed of myself as a woman
for allowing it to get this far,
for waiting for things to get better,
when it was evident
that they wouldn't

i was ashamed,
that i allowed myself
to be with someone who
didn't care about
the fact that they were
slowly ruining me,
that my love for them
was slowly starting to fade

i wish we had never met,
i wish i had waited
for the right person

but at the same time,
i view my pain as a lesson,
a constant reminder
that solely love and affection
don't make a relationship

trusting someone
with your heart
isn't always
the best thing to do

— i should have left him
sooner

why is it
that the road to healing
is so long
after someone
shatters your heart
like glass
leaving you with pain
that is so unbearable
that it leaves you breathless?

— questions i can't answer

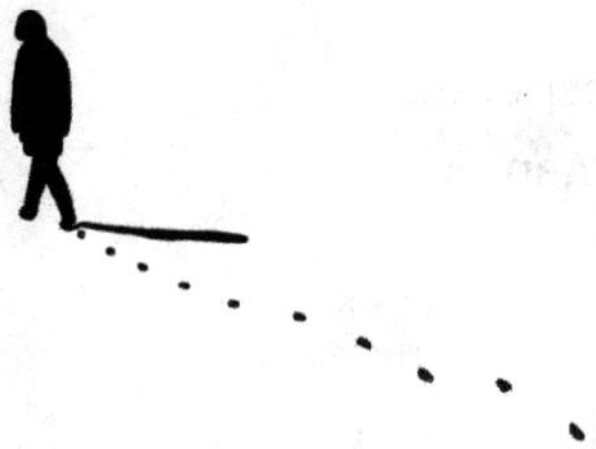

love is a feeling
so universal
yet so unique and intimate...
don't you just hate it?
or am i the only one?

doesn't it just make you cringe?
the heart having desires of its own,
rebelling against the rational mind —
wanting companionship
craving the warmth of another,
needing love...

how painfully desperate
and innately human

— the heart of a human

oh, the twisted game life plays,
causing me to love and trust
the ones that never stay,
forcing me to permanently
care for those
that deliberately
leave me behind

— the aftermath

i am so terrified
of being vulnerable,
of feeling
and acknowledging
that i care
i am afraid
to accept the truth
that while i'm missing you,
you are doing just fine
without me

— the truth hurts

i wish someone
had taught me
how to love

maybe then i wouldn't
be plotting my escape,
for the minute it goes wrong...
assuming it will all go wrong

maybe then i wouldn't
tremble in your hands
at the feel of your touch,
afraid of you

if someone had taught me
how to love
maybe then i would be capable

i lie,
i cheat,
i steal,
i hate,
i lust,
i envy,

but my
greatest
flaw of
all is that
i care

or maybe
it's my best quality —
my superpower

always feeling,
always showing heart

— the real me

i think about you
with deep regret,
knowing i could've saved myself
a heartbreak

i saw you for who you were —
your virtues and vices,
flaws and all
and i accepted your demons
wholeheartedly,

because my heart was tired
of being lonely
my reserved heart
longed for company
and there you were
it was you,
my partner in crime
and i was ready
for us to set the world on fire

that was before
you lit the match
and left me behind
to burn

— blind spot

i am hurting
i feel rejected,
unwanted and unloved
i feel broken
and alone

even when my eyes
leak from devastation
i know i will be okay

time will repair
my shattered heart
i will heal
i will be happy again

i will celebrate
the ones that left me
for their bravery,
for choosing their peace
above all —
even my feelings

— the good in goodbyes

i've never had a lover break my heart
i could never allow it

because i've always known
when to walk away

so unafraid of leaving them behind
that i almost feel guilty

for never allowing myself
to get hurt

that's why i never saw this coming
i never knew that a friend

could break my heart
and devastate my life

how is it possible
the person i bore my soul to,

and shared every mundane detail
of my life with…

could walk out of it
without so much as a goodbye?

but how could i blame you
when it was my own doing

i empowered and emboldened you
with my love,

my trust and my vulnerability
now i pay the price

i live with the deeply engraved scars
of my once shattered heart

— trust gone wrong

i want to thank you
for being yourself
i feel like i owe you so much,
because you gave me everything
you were the perfect storm
a beautiful body of destruction
that cleared my path
showed me what I needed
and all that I deserved

you were perfect
in all your ways
your love was grand,
your lies were impeccable
you made me a believer
you were my sole purpose —
the reason for my existence

when you were present
i was the center of your world
and no one else mattered
until you abandoned me yet again
like I didn't matter

thank you for your dishonesty
because it sharpened
my skill to identify deceptions
thank you for your callousness
that revealed the love i was missing

i could never take you back
because you weren't a devastating loss
the end of us empowered me

to find the love
i could never live without

— the ex i don't regret

if

i were truly broken
and desperately
in need of you

would you still have
abandoned me?

— hypothetically speaking

i eat donuts
when i miss him,
hoping that the taste
will bring back the fond memory
of how he'd feed me donuts
with cherry filling
that he crafted with his hands
whenever i visited
but the memories never appear,
and donuts break my heart
because they remind me of him —
the love forever lost

— souvenirs

i miss who i used to be
i swam in the sea
of optimism
i walked barren trails and made them bloom
i birthed tranquility in the midst of war
i spoke life into desolate people
but that was all before they broke my heart

— the retired alchemist

i wish they could catch
a glimpse of my heart
then they would see me
and comprehend the abyss of my love

but if they saw my heart,

they would never change
because they would know
that i would love
them regardless of their flaws

— shameless heart

i've never cared for eternal life
it seemed like a life filled with boredom
but your love has made me a believer
now i want forever
with you

i want an eternity of arguments
about who's turn it is to do the dishes,
about how unhelpful you are with the kids —
so i want forever
with you

i want grey hairs, wrinkles
and dentures with you
i want laughs with the grandkids
and early bedtimes
i want cliche pastimes,
like cuddles and a movie on saturday nights
i want forever an eternity
with you

— jonathan

when i'm too old to remember my name
i hope that i never forget yours

i hope i'll always remember
that you've been my biggest supporter,
my confidante and friend

i want to remember
your smile
and how you made me laugh

i want to remember
the warmth of your touch
and how you made me feel

i want to remember
that your heart
has held my secrets
and buried my flaws

i hope i never forget
our fights
and how we loved each other
back to oneness

i hope i remember
that in you
i have found the best lover—
my lifetime partner

— the man that loved me right

the mirror

—

the best part
of a day
is the dawn,
when the sun
has yet to rise
and the sky
has remnants
of the night

these are times
when i find
that my imagination
wanders
into unexpected
territory,
and my thoughts
run amok
without anything
to control them
these are times
when my soul
comes alive
and my true being
awakens

i've taken the time
to forgive the people
that have done me wrong,
and thank them
for making me realize
that i deserve better,
and giving me the motivation
to go out and find it

there were days
when i felt so broken
that getting up

every morning
was the last thing
i ever wanted to do

every day
was an opportunity
for my sadness to grow

inside of me
until i could do nothing
but let it to take over

i hid everything
inside myself,
not daring

to let anyone know
how i felt...
shoving my pain

to the farthest depths
of my mind
was one of my greatest skills

but as soon as my day was over
and i found myself alone,
the feelings that i had

locked away
would come flooding back
leaving me in a fit of tears —

a state of emotional pain
that felt like it would never end
it was a book that saved me,

that told me
that i could change my own life
that i could be happy

if i just changed my thoughts
and slowly change my reality
into one where i was happy

so i fought my mind
to replace the angry
negative thoughts

with positive ones
i became kinder to myself
to ease the pain

and slowly,
i became grateful
for being able

to get up,
to see sunlight,
to make it through the day

without feeling sad
it was during those times
that i learned

that my own sadness
was a state
that could only change

if i had the will
to be happy

i asked someone once
if they were proud of me,
if all i had accomplished
in my life
warranted praise
and acknowledgment,

it was that day
that they taught me to
give myself praise first —
even though
i thought less of
my accomplishments
changing my perspective,
giving myself credit,
being proud of myself first,
would make my journey
worth the while

— self-praise

knowledge is so
powerful to me
i could bask in it all day,
learning as much as i can
about anything…
changing my life
and perspective
with just a few books
and advice from others

i crave knowledge,
and i'm grateful for all the
places i can go because of it

— knowledge is power

what does
it feel like
to be happy?

i couldn't
tell you...
the feeling
is so faint,

like a distant
memory
in the back of
my mind
it feels like
i've never been

happiness is
a faraway goal
that i keep
wishing to attain
hoping that
one day
it will
come to me
if i just go
looking for it

i miss the
curly-haired boy
who used to
sit with me
during lunch
in middle school

his eyes
would light up
while he told me
his dreams

and no matter
who told him
he couldn't do it
he'd always find
a way to show them
that he could

i miss the
curly-haired boy
who taught me
how to dream
without limits

— michael the dreamer

all i need,
is a little more time,
a few more hours in the day,
a few more opportunities
to achieve greatness

— chasing the bag

i'm going to find
whatever it is
that makes me whole
and slowly,
i will stitch the broken
inside of me
until i am completely

— leaving it all behind, to
search for myself

the weight
of my decisions
is holding me
hostage,
locking me
in chains
that cannot
be broken
until a
choice is made

i fear the end,
i fear the consequence
of what i choose
if i could,
i would hide

until the
obligation subsides
then maybe,
my burden
would be lifted

i read between
the lines of my life
and i wonder
where is the meaning?
what does it mean
to know
who you are?

i am grateful
for the woman
who saved me

from self-destruction

who caught me
when i fell
close to rock bottom

i'm grateful
for the fact
that my life has
changed because of her
unwavering belief in me

— now it's my turn to save
her

i'm happy with
the way i am,
the way
i turned out

i have decided
that the way
i am now
is a result
of the tears,
the frustration,
the disappointment —
that's part of
the process
of making myself better

— growth

i can't stop thinking
about the past

at times
i find myself
daydreaming,
putting myself
in imaginary situations
where i could have
changed the outcome

but,
i only end up
opening my eyes
to the reality
that i created

— at fault

the worst thing
that i did to myself
was pretend
that my feelings didn't exist

i pushed them
far into the back of my mind
hoping that i would never
have to deal with them
that they would never resurface

and it worked —

or so i thought...

little did i know,
all those feelings would
hit me
all at once,
nearly breaking me
in the process

i tried
to stuff them back in,
they were too much
for me to bear...
the more i tried
the more they surfaced,
tearing me apart

my feelings and i
are in a bitter, raging war
i'm not ready for them,
but they are ready for me

and as of right now,
it looks like
they are winning…

— falling in love with the
forbidden

i struggled
with the concept
of inner peace

drama and a constant
internal battle
seemed to fill my world

having pure, mindful peace
meant that something
was missing
now i know
the true value
of having peace,
of knowing that chaos
does not exist
wherever you are,
that abundance
and prosperity
follow you
wherever you go
solely because
you chose to remove
the negativity,
and distance yourself
from the drama
that never served you

i miss the days
when life
was easy,
when the
only things
i had

to worry about
were what
i was going to eat,
what game
i was going to play
with my friends,
what color
my new sneakers
were going to be...

it's baffling
how much you miss
your childhood
when adulthood becomes
too much to bear

— thoughts of a stressed
adult

if i could go back
to the way it was
the way i felt

the way i needed to be,
would i be better?
would i be enough?

it's as if now
the changes
inside me
are so great

i can't even
fathom the thought
of returning back
to the place
where i
should never be

— growing spiritually

i'm scared of failure,
of not meeting
my own expectations,
of faltering
and having everyone
watch me
when i'm down

i'm scared of the
fact that I'd have to
start all over again
and maybe
when i do that
i'd fail again

or maybe
i'll make it...

either way,
i just don't want to fail

— scared of failure

sometimes,
i lie awake
in my bed at night,
thinking
about the past,

what was —
what could have been...

i wish i could jump
into a time machine
and correct my wrongs,
stop myself
from meeting the people
who brought
chaos and pain
into my life

and then, i wonder...
where would i be now?
would i be any different?
would i be happy?

sometimes,
the past becomes
too much to think about

i have to stop
because the present
is right in front of me

there are
so many possibilities
to find happiness,

to find the people
who will treat me right

but i still consider
my wrongs,
and all those people
who have left me
with wounds
that are still healing
but wouldn't it be nice
to jump
back in time anyway?

why am i waiting
on permission?

the permission
to forgive myself,
the permission to live,
the permission to be free,

why do i
crave the world's
stamp of approval
just to be?

have i no self-esteem?

needing to hear the words
"you are good enough"
from someone other than me

i must end this constant need
for others to validate me

— am i good enough?

the words i often
do not remember
are the praises
of my grandfather

how he'd tell me
that i was going to
change the world,
that there was nothing
that i could not accomplish

because i was brilliant,
the world was mine to conquer
and that there was
an undeniable light within me

but the words
i cannot seem to forget
are the words that left me scarred
the words that dimmed my light,
dwarfed my potential
and shredded my dreams,
words of people i most admired
that told me that
i was not good enough,
or smart enough,
and that i was destined to fail

and every day i wake,
i suit up to slay the dragon
the one they created
with their hateful, hurtful words
but how do i win,

when after i've slain the dragon,
negative self-talk
resurrects him once again?

— the devastating effects of
words

i don't regret the things i've done
or the mistakes i've made
because the lessons were necessary

the things i most profoundly regret
are the things i didn't do
the words i didn't say
the missed opportunities

— there is no bravery in an
inexperienced, unfulfilled
life

i now prioritize my peace of mind above all
i'm present with the people that i cherish
i spend more time doing the things that make me happy

i live like i am deserving of everything good

i love purposefully

i'm aware that i may act differently
that's because i am different
i've found my truest, most authentic self
and i love her!
the change did not break me
but it transformed me
into something beautiful

— butterfly

i have come to the realization
that my greatest flaws are

my heart of gold
and my repairing hands,

determined to save everyone
and fix every broken thing
so determined that i don't realize
not everyone can be saved,
and some things were meant
to be relinquished,
not repurposed

however noble my attempts,
i can't save the world
at the expense of destroying myself

— self preservation

sometimes it's a call
that rocks my world to its core
the sound of your voice
on the other end of the line
with an elaborate heroic story
of how you found your way back to me
and then I tell myself
"i told you so",
because my heart knows better than my head
and my heart knows your heart
that you'd never stay away

sometimes it's an act of fate,
i run into you in the grocery store
of a faraway country
one that we'd never even dreamt of
but we're both there
our eyes meet
and we can't pretend
like we don't recognize
our reflection in each other

now you're ashamed
so you apologize
you tell me that life together was too hard,
that you needed a fresh start
that you'd planned to come back…
but the longer you were away
the more you wanted to stay gone
i'd understand and forgive you
maybe it's desperation
cause i wanted you back

sometimes it's my worst nightmare

that i've finally awakened from,
the years of you gone
were all just a dream
the tears i cried
the sadness that i felt
were all imagined
you were never gone
and i was never alone
i never went years without your smile
i never forgot the sound of your voice
your face never faded from my memory

i daydream many scenarios
of our reunion
because i can't let go —
i don't know how to
i'm haunted by conversations
we did not have,
the places we did not go,
the life we didn't live
because you're gone

i daydream about different scenarios
because my imagination is all i have
anything but the reality
anything but death

there's nothing more empowering than hope,
but nothing more paralyzing

— missing

if happiness is a choice
then why do i feel so unhappy?
i don't recall
ever choosing this
i never wanted depression

but here it is
like a houseguest that refuses to leave
i can't seem to rid myself of
the gloom that envelops me

what if pretending to be happy
is the closest i'll ever get?

— depression

we all desire to be chosen,
it gives us a sense of pride,
reminds us that we hold value
the desire is human nature
and there is nothing wrong with it
as long as we first choose ourselves,
take pride in ourselves
and value ourselves

— i choose me

i don't remember the first time
that i thought about it
i just remember how frequently i did

sadness hijacked my thoughts
suicide felt like my only hope
so i fantasized about the end
every day carried the risk of
ending in a wave of disappointment
and shame for those left behind

how would i go out?
pills, rope, or poison?
i searched the house desperately
but as fate would have it
i lived in a suicide-proof fortress
almost like they knew my thoughts
and made it impenetrable
out of spite
to prolong my suffering

i saw her speeding
she was probably running late for work
after dropping off her son at school
i don't know,
she was minding her business,
going about her life
but i saw her as my opportunity
i was going to walk into her car
and end it all
but my conscience stopped me
"you can't do that to her"
"you can't ruin her life —
it's not right"

"don't hurt her because you're hurting"
of course, my prudish conscience was right
how could i bring her suffering
just to end my own?

i could never decide if i should leave a note
because what was i supposed to say,
"i'm sorry, but...?"
but i wouldn't have been sorry
how could i be?
when i was so miserable that
death seemed like the better alternative
didn't they know that i was in pain?
didn't they see the grief
written in bold on my face?

then again, how could i leave
without a proper goodbye?
how could i deprive
the ones that cared of closure,
leaving them with the pain
that i ran away from?

perhaps, i could tell them
that i was sorry that i hurt them,
that i want them to have the happiness
that i did not,
and that it wasn't their fault...
maybe that would make it all better
i don't remember
when the self-harm thoughts ended
one day they just pack up and left
i no longer prayed for death
i wasn't as hurt or sad anymore

the door of possibility opened
and

i somehow mustered the strength
to crawl through

— the blessing of
unanswered prayers

who broke my mind
to make me feel
so undeserving
of everything

that is good,
unworthy of happiness?

who taught me to think
that i am less-than?

why did i believe them?
or was i always this way,
echoing with
thoughts of inferiority?

unaware of my greatness,
my wholeness,
my worthiness?

ignorant of my potential,
oblivious to the fact
that i am

and always will be
enough

— rewiring

when i become a success story
my thank you speech
will be dedicated
to the j.g.'s of this world;

she is the woman that saw me, a broken girl
and dared to put me back together
by teaching me the importance of resilience and reinvention

— j.g.: an inspirational
woman

why did you raise me this way?
to be authentic
to be assertive and self-assured
to be the voice and not the echo
to do good in the face of evil
to be an asset and not a liability
to embrace difficulty
knowing that nothing worth
achieving comes easy
to always remember who i am
and where i come from
to be a light that
illuminates the darkness
to take up space
and leave my mark on this world

mother,
you taught me well
but your superb wisdom
has left little place for me
in this conformist world

— lessons from mother

i'm attempting to rewrite history
to change the narrative,
reclaim my power,
and stand in my excellence
to love and be loved, wholeheartedly
ceasing the self-sabotage
of believing i'm undeserving
of happiness
and good
i'm releasing thoughts of scarcity
and adopting a mindset of abundance
knowing that the universe
is conspiring on my behalf,
not against me

— my pronoid mind

today, i forgive you for everything —
negative self-talk
lack of self-love and self-compassion
broken promises
things you did not know
things you did not do
giving up too soon
operating beneath your potential
loving the wrong people
not establishing boundaries

you are forgiven
forget the past
embrace the future

— reassess. recenter.
reinvent self

to the person i used to be:

— i forgive you ♡

i'm learning to forgive
people who are not sorry,
and accept the
apologies that never come
because forgiveness is for me —

not them
i forgive for my growth,

peace and happiness
forgiveness is required,

but

reconciliation is optional

— higher self

this is not the life
i thought i'd have
but of course,
i hoped that maybe
i'd be lucky enough
to have a companion
who is love personified,
a home that echos
with joy and laughter,
and a future filled with
amazing possibilities

— dream

be gentle with yourself
because you are not your past mistakes
you are learning and growing,
and growth takes time,
so be patient
you are evolving
and becoming better every day
don't let your past imprison you
free yourself of guilt and shame
but most of all,
love yourself fiercely

— dear self

let's celebrate the ones that never left
the ones that stayed and nurtured us
back from the dead

the ones that gift us their unending love
and unwavering supports

the ones that applaud our geniuses
and betters us with constructive criticisms
the ones that will stay up all night

until we get things right
the ones that pray for our peace,
happiness and prosperity.

may we find them. may we be them.

— tribe

about the authors

— **S.P. Burrell** is an up-and-coming writer in her generation. A native of Jamaica, S.P. started writing at the age of fourteen, beginning work on her first novel "My Name is Edmund" at the age of fifteen, and her devotionals "Live, Love, Conquer", and "Praying for Better" at the age of nineteen. She is a proud musician, realistic artist, photographer, and life coach whose ultimate goal is to inspire as many people as possible with her words.

— **Davia Chin** is a young Philanthropist, Analytical Linguist, emerging Digital Artist, and Higher Education professional. She is the founder of Xaymaca Youth Inspired, Inc., a nonprofit focused on empowering youths in Jamaica and the Caribbean through education, creative arts, and community development. She is a proud wife and mother, passionate about art, music, family, and her home country Jamaica.

CPSIA information can be obtained
at www.ICGtesting.com
Printed in the USA
BVHW052005090921
616447BV00009B/185